Contents

General Knowledge – page 2
Transfers 2000-2009 – page 6
Cup Games – page 10
Memorable Games – page 12
Memorable Goals – page 14
Red Cards – page 16
Managers – page 19
First Goals – page 21
Transfers 2010-2021 - page 27

General Knowledge Answers – page 32
Transfers 2000-2009 Answers – page 36
Cup Games Answers – page 41
Memorable Games Answers – page 44
Memorable Goals Answers – page 47
Red Cards Answers – page 50
Managers Answers – page 53
First Goals Answers – page 55
Transfers 2010-2021 Answers – page 59

General Knowledge

1) Who scored the first goal for Ipswich Town in the 21st Century in the 2-1 away win at Port Vale in January 2000?

2) Who was the Ipswich main shirt sponsor for the first season back in the Premier League for the 2000/01 season?

3) Against which club did Andre Dozzell make his Ipswich debut?

4) Who was the clubs top scorer in the 2006/07 Championship season with 16 goals?

5) Which team beat Ipswich in the Championship Play-Off Semi Final in both 2004 and 2005?

6) Who became the first player from Mauritius to represent the club when he signed in 2014?

7) Connor Wickham made his debut aged 16 years and 11 days against which team in 2009?

8) Ipswich were relegated from the Premier League in 2002 following defeat on the last day to which team?

9) Which two teams were relegated alongside Ipswich that season?

10) What shirt number did Emyr Huws wear throughout his time at the club?

11) Who did Luke Chambers replace as club captain in 2014?

12) Which Shrewsbury player scored an own goal to help Ipswich turn the game around to earn a 2-1 win in November 2020?

13) How many games did Ipswich win throughout the Championship season in 2018/19 as they were relegated to League One?

14) Which goalkeeper earned Ipswich a point by saving a penalty in the 0-0 draw with Wimbledon in April 2021?

15) Who scored the final penalty in the shoot-out win over Peterborough in the EFL Trophy in 2019?

16) Which county did England beat 3-1 in a friendly at Portman Road in 2003?

17) Who scored a hat-trick against Barnsley on the opening day of the 2016/17 season after coming on at half time?

18) Which club did Richard Wright play for in between his second and third spells at Ipswich?

19) In what year did Marcus Evans first become the majority shareholder in the club?

20) Which club did Jim Magilton make his final appearance as a player against in April 2006?

Transfers 2000-2009

1) From which club did Ipswich buy Marcus Stewart in February 2000?

2) Which defender arrived on a free transfer from Tottenham in July 2000?

3) From which team did Ipswich purchase Hermann Hreidarsson in August 2000?

4) David Johnson was sold to which side in January 2001?

5) Which forward arrived from Mallorca in August 2001?

6) Which goalkeeper was sold to Arsenal in July 2001?

7) Which player was sold to Newcastle in July 2002?

8) Who left to join Charlton in June 2003?

9) Which striker joined on a free from Sheffield Wednesday in November 2003?

10) Marcus Bent was sold to which Premier League team in June 2004?

11) Darren Currie was bought from where in December 2004?

12) Ipswich sold which goalkeeper to Sunderland in June 2005?

13) Which striker joined on a free transfer from Reading in June 2005?

14) James Scowcroft joined which team after leaving Ipswich in July 2005?

15) Which winger joined from Newcastle in August 2006?

16) From which lower league side was Jonathan Walters bought in January 2007?

17) Which player left to join Leeds in the deal which saw Dan Harding move the other way in August 2006?

18) Pablo Counago returned to Ipswich in July 2007 after leaving which Spanish side?

19) Gareth McAuley was signed by Ipswich from which team?

20) Neil Alexander move to which Scottish team in January 2008?

21) From which club was Kevin Lisbie purchased in July 2008?

22) Which experienced midfielder joined on a free from Bolton in August 2008?

23) Tommy Miller was sold to which club in May 2009?

24) Which player joined on a free from Manchester United in July 2009?

25) Which two players joined from Sunderland in September 2009?

Cup Games

1) Which Ipswich player scored the winner in extra time to beat Manchester City in the League Cup Quarter Final in December 2000?

2) Who scored the late equaliser in the UEFA Cup First Round home leg against Torpedo Moscow in September 2001?

3) Which club did Ipswich knock out of the UEFA Cup in the Second Round in 2001?

4) Who scored both Ipswich goals in the 4-2 aggregate defeat to Inter Milan in the UEFA Cup in 2001?

5) Which club knocked Ipswich out of the UEFA Cup in 2002?

6) Which team did Ipswich knock out of the FA Cup at the Fourth Round stage in January 2007?

7) By what score did Chelsea beat Ipswich in the FA Cup Third Round in 2011?

8) Who scored the only goal as Ipswich won the first leg of their League Cup Semi Final against Arsenal in 2011?

9) By what aggregate score-line did Ipswich ultimately lose that Semi Final tie?

10) Who did Ipswich knock out the FA Cup in the First Round in September 2019?

11) Which was the only team that Ipswich beat in the EFL Trophy in the 2020/21 competition?

12) Between 2011 and 2021 how many times did Ipswich get past the Third Round of the FA Cup?

Memorable Games

1) Who scored the only goal as Ipswich claimed victory over Liverpool at Anfield in December 2000?

2) What was the score in the home leg of the UEFA Cup qualifying game against FC Avenir Beggen in 2002?

3) Which two players scored in the 2-0 victory over Norwich in March 2003?

4) Who scored by lobbing the keeper to give Ipswich a last-minute 4-3 win away at Crystal Palace in October 2003?

5) Ipswich beat Burnley by what score-line at home in the First Division in October 2003?

6) Which Championship team did Ipswich beat 6-0 at home in March 2005?

7) Who came off the bench to score twice in the 3-1 win over Norwich in November 2006?

8) What was the final score in the derby victory over Norwich in April 2009?

9) Connor Wickham scored a hat trick away from home in a 6-0 victory over which team in February 2011?

10) Richard Chaplow bagged a last minute goal to steal a 1-0 win away at which team in March 2015?

11) Who netted in the last minute to give Ipswich a 2-1 victory over Reading in February 2016?

12) Which team did Ipswich beat 3-2 in their last game in the Championship in May 2019?

Memorable Goals

1) Who put Ipswich 1-0 up away to Spurs in their first Premier League game in August 2000 before they fell to a 3-1 defeat?

2) Who scored twice, including with an incredible long-range left footed volley against Bolton in the first leg of the 2000 Play-Off Semi Final?

3) Who scored a consolation goal with a 30 yard dipping effort in the 3-2 home loss to West Ham in October 2001?

4) Finidi George lobbed the onrushing goalkeeper in the December 2001 Premier League meeting with which club?

5) Jimmy Bullard scored with an angled drive and free kick in the 2-0 away win over which team in March 2011?

6) David McGoldrick curled in a free-kick from the edge of the box in a 1-1 draw with which team in October 2014?

7) Who scored a 95th minute winner on his debut to claim a 1-0 win away at Charlton in November 2014?

8) Which loan player cut in from the left against Preston before rifling in a stunning goal in January 2017?

9) Which player scored with a scorching left footed volley in the 3-1 win over Newcastle in April 2017?

10) Who curled in a left footed free kick to open the scoring in the 3-0 win over Preston in November 2017?

11) James Norwood scored with a beautiful lob from the edge of the area in a 4-1 win over which team in January 2020?

Red Cards

1) Marcus Stewart was controversially sent off against which team in the Premier League in February 2001?

2) Which goalkeeper was dismissed against Leicester in September 2001, although later had the red card overturned on appeal?

3) Ipswich came from 2-0 down to beat Plymouth 3-2 in September 2004 despite seeing which player be dismissed in the first half?

4) Castro Sito was sent off twice in one week in September 2005 against which two Championship sides?

5) Who was given his marching orders following a confrontation with Derby goalkeeper Stephen Bywater in April 2007?

6) Which Ipswich player was dismissed for a professional foul during the 4-1 loss to Norwich in November 2010?

7) Which two Ipswich players were shown red cards during the 7-1 hammering by Peterborough in August 2011?

8) Aaron Cresswell was sent off late on in the 1-1 draw with which team in November 2013?

9) Jordan Spence saw red in a Championship clash with which club in January 2018?

10) Who received two yellow cards in the 1-0 away victory over Fleetwood in October 2019?

11) Who was sent off in the 2-1 defeat away at Sunderland in November 2020?

12) Kayden Jackson was shown a straight red for a reckless challenge against which team in January 2021?

13) Referee Darren Drysdale sent off which Ipswich player during the 0-0 draw with Northampton Town in February 2021?

Managers

1) Who was Ipswich Town manager at the beginning of the 21st Century?

2) Against which team did Paul Cook register his first win as Ipswich boss?

3) Who took over as manager after Roy Keane left the club?

4) How many games did Paul Hurst win out of his 15 games as Ipswich manager?

5) How many points did Ipswich take in Paul Lambert's last four games as manager?

6) Which team did Joe Royle face in his first game as Ipswich manager?

7) What was the result in Jim Magilton's last game in charge of the club?

8) Who was the manager as the club were relegated from the Championship in 2019?

9) Who became caretaker manager after Roy Keane left the club in 2011?

10) What was the clubs highest league finish under the management of Mick McCarthy?

First Goals

Can you name the club that these players scored their first goal for Ipswich against?

1) Marcus Stewart
   a) **Bolton**
   b) **Bristol City**
   c) **Barnsley**

2) Titus Bramble
   a) **Sunderland**
   b) **Newcastle**
   c) **Middlesbrough**

3) Darren Ambrose
   a) **Colchester**
   b) **Walsall**
   c) **Crystal Palace**

4) Pablo Counago
   a) **Derby County**
   b) **West Brom**
   c) **Leicester City**

5) Finidi George
   a) Derby County
   b) Manchester City
   c) Blackburn Rovers

6) Darren Bent
   a) Newcastle United
   b) West Ham
   c) Tottenham

7) Shefki Kuqi
   a) Wolves
   b) Watford
   c) Everton

8) Sam Parkin
   a) QPR
   b) West Brom
   c) Fulham

9) Jonathan Walters
   a) Portsmouth
   b) Stoke
   c) QPR

10) Jon Stead
   a) **Reading**
   b) **Fulham**
   c) **Millwall**

11) Ivan Campo
   a) **Barnsley**
   b) **Leeds**
   c) **Sheffield Wednesday**

12) Carlos Edwards
   a) **Sheffield Wednesday**
   b) **Millwall**
   c) **Sunderland**

13) Jimmy Bullard
   a) **Wigan**
   b) **Derby County**
   c) **Blackburn**

14) Christophe Berra
   a) **Birmingham City**
   b) **Leicester City**
   c) **Wolves**

15) Tyrone Mings
   a) **Birmingham City**
   b) **Bournemouth**
   c) **Sunderland**

16) David McGoldrick
   a) **Sheffield United**
   b) **Fulham**
   c) **Middlesbrough**

17) Luke Chambers
   a) **QPR**
   b) **Sheffield United**
   c) **Huddersfield**

18) Daryl Murphy
   a) **Norwich**
   b) **Middlesbrough**
   c) **Blackburn**

19) Freddie Sears
   a) **Brighton**
   b) **Portsmouth**
   c) **West Ham**

20) Brett Pitman
   a) **Preston North End**
   b) **Bournemouth**
   c) **Derby County**

21) Andre Dozzell
   a) **Rotherham**
   b) **Sheffield Wednesday**
   c) **QPR**

22) Kayden Jackson
   a) **Exeter City**
   b) **Colchester**
   c) **Coventry City**

23) Alan Judge
   a) **Oldham Athletic**
   b) **Southend**
   c) **Lincoln City**

24) Will Keane
   a) **Rotherham**
   b) **Sunderland**
   c) **Lincoln City**

25) Luke Woolfenden
    a) **Lincoln City**
    b) **Wimbledon**
    c) **Oxford United**

Transfers 2010-2021

1) Which player arrived from Luton in the January transfer window in 2011?

2) Which club did Michael Chopra join from in June 2011?

3) Who did Alex Bruce sign for after leaving in August 2010?

4) Which midfielder arrived on a free from Birmingham City in July 2011?

5) Connor Wickham was sold to which club in the summer of 2011?

6) Which player was bought from Colchester in January 2013?

7) Nigel Reo-Coker signed for which team after leaving Ipswich in 2013?

8) Which three players signed on free transfers from Bristol City in July 2013?

9) Which club did Carlos Edwards move to from Ipswich in May 2014?

10) Which player was signed from Borussia Dortmund in July 2014?

11) Goalkeeper Paddy Kenny signed from which club in January 2015?

12) Who was sold to West Ham in July 2014?

13) Which striker arrived from Bournemouth in June 2015?

14) From which club did Ipswich sign Kevin Foley in 2016?

15) Tyrone Mings was sold to which team in June 2015?

16) Kieffer Moore was bought from where in the 2017 winter transfer window?

17) Which player left to join Newcastle in August 2016?

18) Which forward was sold to Rangers in August 2017?

19) Which young player left the club to join Celtic in July 2017?

20) Ipswich signed which two players from Shrewsbury in August 2018?

21) Which club did Kevin Bru join on a free after leaving in July 2018?

22) Ipswich brought in Kane Vincent-Young from which club in August 2019?

23) Jordan Spence left to join which Dutch club in 2020?

24) Which player arrived from Stoke City in August 2020?

25) Which player joined Colchester on a free transfer after leaving Ipswich in June 2021?

Answers

General Knowledge Answers

1) Who scored the first goal for Ipswich Town in the 21st Century in the 2-1 away win at Port Vale in January 2000?
Matt Holland

2) Who was the Ipswich main shirt sponsor for the first season back in the Premier League for the 2000/01 season?
Greene King

3) Against which club did Andre Dozzell make his Ipswich debut?
Sheffield Wednesday

4) Who was the clubs top scorer in the 2006/07 Championship season with 16 goals?
Alan Lee

5) Which team beat Ipswich in the Championship Play-Off Semi Final in both 2004 and 2005?
West Ham

6) Who became the first player from Mauritius to represent the club when he signed in 2014?
Kevin Bru

7) Connor Wickham made his debut aged 16 years and 11 days against which team in 2009?
Doncaster Rovers

8) Ipswich were relegated from the Premier League in 2002 following defeat on the last day to which team?
Liverpool

9) Which two teams were relegated alongside Ipswich that season?
Leicester City and Derby County

10) What shirt number did Emyr Huws wear throughout his time at the club?
44

11) Who did Luke Chambers replace as club captain in 2014?
Carlos Edwards

12) Which Shrewsbury player scored an own goal to help Ipswich turn the game around to earn a 2-1 win in November 2020?
Ethan Ebanks-Landell

13) How many games did Ipswich win throughout the Championship season in 2018/19 as they were relegated to League One?
Five

14) Which goalkeeper earned Ipswich a point by saving a penalty in the 0-0 draw with Wimbledon in April 2021?
David Cornell

15) Who scored the final penalty in the shoot-out win over Peterborough in the EFL Trophy in 2019?
Barry Cotter

16) Which county did England beat 3-1 in a friendly at Portman Road in 2003?
Croatia

17) Who scored a hat-trick against Barnsley on the opening day of the 2016/17 season after coming on at half time?
Grant Ward

18) Which club did Richard Wright play for in between his second and third spells at Ipswich?
Sheffield United

19) In what year did Marcus Evans first become the majority shareholder in the club?
2007

20) Which club did Jim Magilton make his final appearance as a player against in April 2006?
Plymouth Argyle

Transfers 2000-2009 Answers

1) From which club did Ipswich buy Marcus Stewart in February 2000?
Huddersfield Town

2) Which defender arrived on a free transfer from Tottenham in July 2000?
John Scales

3) From which team did Ipswich purchase Hermann Hreidarsson in August 2000?
Wimbledon

4) David Johnson was sold to which side in January 2001?
Nottingham Forest

5) Which forward arrived from Mallorca in August 2001?
Finidi George

6) Which goalkeeper was sold to Arsenal in July 2001?
Richard Wright

7) Which player was sold to Newcastle in July 2002?
Titus Bramble

8) Who left to join Charlton in June 2003?
Matt Holland

9) Which striker joined on a free from Sheffield Wednesday in November 2003?
Shefki Kuqi

10) Marcus Bent was sold to which Premier League team in June 2004?
Everton

11) Darren Currie was bought from where in December 2004?
Brighton

12) Ipswich sold which goalkeeper to Sunderland in June 2005?
Kelvin Davis

13) Which striker joined on a free transfer from Reading in June 2005?
Nicky Forster

14) James Scowcroft joined which team after leaving Ipswich in July 2005?
Coventry City

15) Which winger joined from Newcastle in August 2006?
Martin Brittain

16) From which lower league side was Jonathan Walters bought in January 2007?
Chester City

17) Which player left to join Leeds in the deal which saw Dan Harding move the other way in August 2006?
Ian Westlake

18) Pablo Counago returned to Ipswich in July 2007 after leaving which Spanish side?
Malaga

19) Gareth McAuley was signed by Ipswich from which team?
Leicester City

20) Neil Alexander move to which Scottish team in January 2008?
Rangers

21) From which club was Kevin Lisbie purchased in July 2008?
Colchester United

22) Which experienced midfielder joined on a free from Bolton in August 2008?
Ivan Campo

23) Tommy Miller was sold to which club in May 2009?
Sheffield Wednesday

24) Which player joined on a free from Manchester United in July 2009?
Lee Martin

25) Which two players joined from Sunderland in September 2009?
Grant Leadbitter and Carlos Edwards

Cup Games Answers

1) Which Ipswich player scored the winner in extra time to beat Manchester City in the League Cup Quarter Final in December 2000?
Mark Venus

2) Who scored the late equaliser in the UEFA Cup First Round home leg against Torpedo Moscow in September 2001?
Titus Bramble

3) Which club did Ipswich knock out of the UEFA Cup in the Second Round in 2001?
Helsingborgs

4) Who scored both Ipswich goals in the 4-2 aggregate defeat to Inter Milan in the UEFA Cup in 2001?
Alun Armstrong

5) Which club knocked Ipswich out of the UEFA Cup in 2002?
Slovan Liberec

6) Which team did Ipswich knock out of the FA Cup at the Fourth Round stage in January 2007?
Swansea

7) By what score did Chelsea beat Ipswich in the FA Cup Third Round in 2011?
7-0

8) Who scored the only goal as Ipswich won the first leg of their League Cup Semi Final against Arsenal in 2011?
Tamas Priskin

9) By what aggregate score-line did Ipswich ultimately lose that Semi Final tie?
3-1

10) Who did Ipswich knock out the FA Cup in the First Round in September 2019?
Lincoln City

11) Which was the only team that Ipswich beat in the EFL Trophy in the 2020/21 competition?
Gillingham

12) Between 2011 and 2021 how many times did Ipswich get past the Third Round of the FA Cup?
Zero

Memorable Games Answers

1) Who scored the only goal as Ipswich claimed victory over Liverpool at Anfield in December 2000?
Marcus Stewart

2) What was the score in the home leg of the UEFA Cup qualifying game against FC Avenir Beggen in 2002?
8-1

3) Which two players scored in the 2-0 victory over Norwich in March 2003?
Fabian Wilnis and Darren Bent

4) Who scored by lobbing the keeper to give Ipswich a last-minute 4-3 win away at Crystal Palace in October 2003?
Shefki Kuqi

5) Ipswich beat Burnley by what score-line at home in the First Division in October 2003?
6-1

6) Which Championship team did Ipswich beat 6-0 at home in March 2005?
Nottingham Forest

7) Who came off the bench to score twice in the 3-1 win over Norwich in November 2006?
Danny Haynes

8) What was the final score in the derby victory over Norwich in April 2009?
3-2

9) Connor Wickham scored a hat trick away from home in a 6-0 victory over which team in February 2011?
Doncaster

10) Richard Chaplow bagged a last minute goal to steal a 1-0 win away at which team in March 2015?
Watford

11) Who netted in the last minute to give Ipswich a 2-1 victory over Reading in February 2016?
Brett Pitman

12) Which team did Ipswich beat 3-2 in their last game in the Championship in May 2019?
Leeds United

Memorable Goals Answers

1) Who put Ipswich 1-0 up away to Spurs in their first Premier League game in August 2000 before they fell to a 3-1 defeat?
Mark Venus

2) Who scored twice, including with an incredible long-range left footed volley against Bolton in the first leg of the 2000 Play-Off Semi Final?
Marcus Stewart

3) Who scored a consolation goal with a 30 yard dipping effort in the 3-2 home loss to West Ham in October 2001?
Matt Holland

4) Finidi George lobbed the onrushing goalkeeper in the December 2001 Premier League meeting with which club?
Sunderland

5) Jimmy Bullard scored with an angled drive and free kick in the 2-0 away win over which team in March 2011?
Cardiff

6) David McGoldrick curled in a free-kick from the edge of the box in a 1-1 draw with which team in October 2014?
Blackburn Rovers

7) Who scored a 95th minute winner on his debut to claim a 1-0 win away at Charlton in November 2014?
Noel Hunt

8) Which loan player cut in from the left against Preston before rifling in a stunning goal in January 2017?
Tom Lawrence

9) Which player scored with a scorching left footed volley in the 3-1 win over Newcastle in April 2017?
Emyr Huws

10) Who curled in a left footed free kick to open the scoring in the 3-0 win over Preston in November 2017?
Martyn Waghorn

11) James Norwood scored with a beautiful lob from the edge of the area in a 4-1 win over which team in January 2020?
Accrington Stanley

Red Cards Answers

1) Marcus Stewart was controversially sent off against which team in the Premier League in February 2001?
Leeds United

2) Which goalkeeper was dismissed against Leicester in September 2001, although later had the red card overturned on appeal?
Matteo Sereni

3) Ipswich came from 2-0 down to beat Plymouth 3-2 in September 2004 despite seeing which player be dismissed in the first half?
Fabian Wilnis

4) Castro Sito was sent off twice in one week in September 2005 against which two Championship sides?
Sheffield United and Norwich City

5) Who was given his marching orders following a confrontation with Derby goalkeeper Stephen Bywater in April 2007?
Alex Bruce

6) Which Ipswich player was dismissed for a professional foul during the 4-1 loss to Norwich in November 2010?
Damien Delaney

7) Which two Ipswich players were shown red cards during the 7-1 hammering by Peterborough in August 2011?
Lee Martin and Tommy Smith

8) Aaron Cresswell was sent off late on in the 1-1 draw with which team in November 2013?
Barnsley

9) Jordan Spence saw red in a Championship clash with which club in January 2018?
Fulham

10) Who received two yellow cards in the 1-0 away victory over Fleetwood in October 2019?
James Wilson

11) Who was sent off in the 2-1 defeat away at Sunderland in November 2020?
Andre Dozzell

12) Kayden Jackson was shown a straight red for a reckless challenge against which team in January 2021?
Sunderland

13) Referee Darren Drysdale sent off which Ipswich player during the 0-0 draw with Northampton Town in February 2021?
Flynn Downes

Managers Answers

1) Who was Ipswich Town manager at the beginning of the 21st Century?
George Burley

2) Against which team did Paul Cook register his first win as Ipswich boss?
Plymouth

3) Who took over as manager after Roy Keane left the club?
Paul Jewell

4) How many games did Paul Hurst win out of his 15 games as Ipswich manager?
One

5) How many points did Ipswich take in Paul Lambert's last four games as manager?
Eight

6) Which team did Joe Royle face in his first game as Ipswich manager?
Slovan Liberec

7) What was the result in Jim Magilton's last game in charge of the club?
Ipswich 3-2 Norwich

8) Who was the manager as the club were relegated from the Championship in 2019?
Paul Lambert

9) Who became caretaker manager after Roy Keane left the club in 2011?
Ian McParland

10) What was the clubs highest league finish under the management of Mick McCarthy?
6th in the Championship

First Goals Answers

1) Marcus Stewart
   Barnsley

2) Titus Bramble
   Sunderland

3) Darren Ambrose
   Walsall

4) Pablo Counago
   Leicester City

5) Finidi George
   Derby County

6) Darren Bent
   Newcastle United

7) Shefki Kuqi
   Watford

8) Sam Parkin
   QPR

9) Jonathan Walters
   QPR

10) Jon Stead
    Reading

11) Ivan Campo
    Barnsley

12) Carlos Edwards
    Sheffield Wednesday

13) Jimmy Bullard
    Derby County

14) Christophe Berra
    Birmingham City

15) Tyrone Mings
    Birmingham City

16) David McGoldrick
Middlesbrough

17) Luke Chambers
Huddersfield

18) Daryl Murphy
Middlesbrough

19) Freddie Sears
Brighton

20) Brett Pitman
Preston North End

21) Andre Dozzell
Sheffield Wednesday

22) Kayden Jackson
Exeter City

23) Alan Judge
Lincoln City

24) Will Keane

Rotherham

25) Luke Woolfenden

Lincoln City

Transfers 2010-2021 Answers

1) Which player arrived from Luton in the January transfer window in 2011?
Andy Drury

2) Which club did Michael Chopra join from in June 2011?
Cardiff

3) Who did Alex Bruce sign for after leaving in August 2010?
Leeds United

4) Which midfielder arrived on a free from Birmingham City in July 2011?
Lee Bowyer

5) Connor Wickham was sold to which club in the summer of 2011?
Sunderland

6) Which player was bought from Colchester in January 2013?
Anthony Wordsworth

7) Nigel Reo-Coker signed for which team after leaving Ipswich in 2013?
Vancouver Whitecaps

8) Which three players signed on free transfers from Bristol City in July 2013?
Cole Skuse, Paul Anderson and Dean Gerken

9) Which club did Carlos Edwards move to from Ipswich in May 2014?
Millwall

10) Which player was signed from Borussia Dortmund in July 2014?
Balint Bajner

11) Goalkeeper Paddy Kenny signed from which club in January 2015?
Bolton

12) Who was sold to West Ham in July 2014?
Aaron Cresswell

13) Which striker arrived from Bournemouth in June 2015?
Brett Pitman

14) From which club did Ipswich sign Kevin Foley in 2016?
FC Copenhagen

15) Tyrone Mings was sold to which team in June 2015?
Bournemouth

16) Kieffer Moore was bought from where in the 2017 winter transfer window?
Forest Green

17) Which player left to join Newcastle in August 2016?
Daryl Murphy

18) Which forward was sold to Rangers in August 2017?
Martyn Waghorn

19) Which young player left the club to join Celtic in July 2017?
Kundai Benyu

20) Ipswich signed which two players from Shrewsbury in August 2018?
Jon Nolan and Aristote Nsiala

21) Which club did Kevin Bru join on a free after leaving in July 2018?
Apollon Limassol

22) Ipswich brought in Kane Vincent-Young from which club in August 2019?
Colchester

23) Jordan Spence left to join which Dutch club in 2020?
ADO Den Haag

24) Which player arrived from Stoke City in August 2020?
Stephen Ward

25) Which player joined Colchester on a free transfer after leaving Ipswich in June 2021?

Alan Judge

If you enjoyed this book please consider leaving a five star review on Amazon

Books by Jack Pearson available on Amazon:

Cricket:

Cricket World Cup 2019 Quiz Book
The Ashes 2019 Cricket Quiz Book
The Ashes 2010-2019 Quiz Book
The Ashes 2005 Quiz Book
The Indian Premier League Quiz Book

Football:

The Quiz Book of the England Football Team in the 21st Century
The Quiz Book of Arsenal Football Club in the 21st Century
The Quiz Book of Aston Villa Football Club in the 21st Century
The Quiz Book of Chelsea Football Club in the 21st Century

The Quiz Book of Everton Football Club in the 21st Century

The Quiz Book of Leeds United Football Club in the 21st Century

The Quiz Book of Leicester City Football Club in the 21st Century

The Quiz Book of Liverpool Football Club in the 21st Century

The Quiz Book of Manchester City Football Club in the 21st Century

The Quiz Book of Manchester United Football Club in the 21st Century

The Quiz Book of Newcastle United Football Club in the 21st Century

The Quiz Book of Southampton Football Club in the 21st Century

The Quiz Book of Sunderland Association Football Club in the 21st Century

The Quiz Book of Tottenham Hotspur Football Club in the 21st Century

The Quiz Book of West Ham United Football Club in the 21st Century

The Quiz Book of Wrexham Association Football Club in the 21st Century

Printed in Great Britain
by Amazon

18459286R00037